Northamptonshire
in Pictures

To / SYLVIA

WITH LOVE FROM

TOM AND CAROL

MAY 2010

at heart ♡ publications
www.atheart.co.uk

Telegraph
EVENING

First published in 2008 by
At Heart Ltd
32 Stamford Street
Altrincham
Cheshire
WA14 1EY

in conjunction with
Northamptonshire Evening Telegraph
Ise Park
Rothwell Road
Kettering
NN16 8GA

ISBN: 978-1-84547-203-0

Printed and bound by Ashford Colour Press, Gosport.

CONTENTS

Tala, a Staffie pup, aged seven months

Caroline Chapman, Kettering, with her winning picture

Birds on Corby Boating Lake
Michael Mahon, Corby

Sleeping cat called Jupiter
Melanie Page, Higham Ferrers

Ducks at Wicksteed Park
Sara Simms, Kettering

Dogs enjoying themselves on a roundabout
Mavis Howden, Great Oakley

Off for a wander, Wicksteed Park
Sara Simms, Kettering

Lapland Walk, Danesholme
Robert Scott, Danesholme, Corby

Swan in the mist, Denford
Lynne Brice, Kettering

Autumn, our pet dog
Kevin Emsley, Corby

New Year's Day 2008, Fotheringhay
Church, near Oundle
Lucy Angus, Kettering

Llamas at Loddington
Ray Fox, Barton Seagrave

The dog admires sunset
Gary Evans, Finedon

A red kite above the house
Karl Hannant, Kettering

Our two dogs, Ollie and Alex
Michelle Kowalski, Stoneygate, Leicester

Spirit and Sandringham
Fred Jefferson, Thrapston

My dog, Silver
Crystal Dziarkowska, Corby

Long tailed tit outside the
house, Grafton Underwood
Karl Hannant, Kettering

My Nanna's dog
Kelly Smith, Wellingborough

My dogs, Honey and Sophie
Kerrianne Burgess, Wellingborough

14

Tiggy, our dog
Helen Plowman, Kettering

At home, February 2007
Jonathan James, Broughton

Our cat, Sparky
Jim Tomlin, Corby

In the garden, August 2006
James Stewart, Higham Ferrers

Swans at the embankment,
Wellingborough, January 2008
Julian Greenwood, Kettering

Hettie takes 40 winks
Samantha Jones, Irchester

Little and Large
Linda Eady, Wollaston

Jake, six, looks amazed at this frosty
spider's web on his playhouse
Tracy Sheridan, Corby

Penny, on Christmas morning
Ling Cheung, Corby

Common frog on a toadstool,
Corby, Summer 2007
Lisa Joy Oliver, Corby

Heron on top of a house in
Harrington Road, Rothwell
K.M. Briggs, Rothwell

Our back garden last summer
Donna McEneaney, Kettering

Orange slug in my garden
Ruth Plumley, Burton Latimer

My deaf white cat, Google-Eye
Priska Wichmann, Finedon

My dog, Chelsea, in the garden
Dru Hollies-Cox, Northampton

Our dog, Christmas Day 2006
Nicola Perrin, Rothwell

A friendly squirrel in our back garden
Phyl Davies, Rushden

Coming in to land at Pitsford Reservoir
Jade Hurst, Wellingborough

An owl looking whimsical
Steve Bryan, Kettering

Luca (left) and Charlie, posing in the garden
Peter McDonald, Corby

Jerry the horse
Sarah Watson

A wren
Grahame Allen, Irthlingborough

A frog
Grahame Allen, Irthlingborough

A squirrel, East Carlton
Stephen Martin

A wasp in my garden,
October time
Ry Brice, Kettering

Jerry the cat
Rebecca Wildman, Barton Seagrave, Kettering

Butterfly at Rutland Water
Danni Thompson, Desborough

Ducklings, Grafton Underwood
Carlene Byland, Kettering

A frog in my garden
Diana Railton, Woodford

Teezer the cat
Alan Savage, Rushden

At the village of Sywell
Robert Coles, Little Harrowden

Pybald ponies near Salcey Forest
Dave Clarke, Hardingstone

Family likeness near Blatherwycke village
Robert Coles, Little Harrowden

My cat, Jack, July 2006
Marina Kraan, Corby

Corby Boating Lake,
October 2007
Marina Kraan, Corby

Scrabble and Bob
Diana Railton, Woodford

A frog in my garden pond
Susan Crick, Desborough

Swans at Wicksteed Park
Julia Humphries, Barton Seagrave

Caged wildlife
Nola Rich, Raunds

Stanwick Lakes
Geoff Hayward, Barton Seagrave

Rabbits on the old Cranford branch line
J.D. Ashby, Kettering

Horses at Broughton Grange
Lynne Brice, Kettering

A swan on the river
at Wharf Road
Jim McCall,
Higham Ferrers

A swan at sunset, Denford
on Christmas Day 2007
Ry Brice, Kettering

Tigger, the Bengal kitten
Janet Cross, Thrapston

Molly, a five-month-old cocker spaniel
Claire Bland, Wellingborough

A dog swimming at Wicksteed Park back lake
J.D. Ashby, Kettering

Swan at Denford, October 2007
Ry Brice, Kettering

A scottie dog, Holly, among
the forget-me-nots
Jenny Barker, Pytchley

Grass snakes at Wicksteed Park
J.D. Ashby, Kettering

Waiting for my dinner
S. Brocklehurst, Irthlingborough

A terrapin and coot, Wicksteed backwater
John Ashby, Kettering

Swan Lake, taken at Stanwick Lakes
Pat Weedy, Higham Ferrers

Polperro out to sea, August 2007

Samantha Jones, Irchester, with her winning picture

Thrapston Yachting Club
Valerie Jefferson, Thrapston

A rainbow arches over
Barton Seagrave
Ray Fox, Barton Seagrave

47

Geddington Bridge,
Christmas Day
Thomas Bailey

Early one morning in July at Lyveden New Bield
Sylvia Adams, Brigstock, Corby

Salcey Forest looking down from
the tree top walk, Autumn 2007
Lucy Angus, Kettering

Snowy day in Desborough
Kathy Crisp, Desborough

Taken at Kelmarsh Hall, February 2008
Mike Camp, Thrapston

Sunset at Denford
Lynne Brice, Kettering

50

Wicksteed Park
Sara Simms, Kettering

Fotheringhay Church, near Oundle, New Year's Day 2008
Lucy Angus, Kettering

51

Wicksteed Park, Kettering, Autumn 2007
Lydia Hover, Kettering

Althorp House
Sara Simms, Kettering

Boat on the water at the Pitsford Reservoir
Kathy Crisp, Desborough

Lyveden New Bield, near Oundle
Kevin O'Brien, Desborough

Snow drops at East Carlton Park
Kevin Emsley, Corby

Ise Valley in Kettering, after
the flooding of the river
Julian Sanders, Kettering

Cransley
Kevin Emsley, Corby

Sunrise over Warkton Lake
Liz Pegg, Kettering

Steam train over Harringworth Viaduct
Kevin O'Brien, Desborough

58

Daventry Country Park
Michal Cieszczyk, Kettering

Salcey Forest
Marjorie Bosworth, Kettering

Misty glade, Slipton
Steve Bryan, Kettering

Trees on a foggy day beside
Great Oakley Cricket Club
Margaret Hay, Corby

60

Wescott Way, Corby, February 2008
Lorraine Dziarkowska, Corby

Wescott Way, Corby, February 2008
Lorraine Dziarkowska, Corby

Wicksteed Park, December 2007
Steve Coe, Wellingborough

My road in the snow
Craig Hodge, Raunds

Grafton Underwood
Jamie Mckerral, Kettering

A duck on the lake at Sywell Country Park
Kelly Smith, Wellingborough

64

Dawn from our back door
Penny Mahoney, Kettering

Isham Mill
Keith Smile

65

Geddington bridge at night
Jamie Mckerral, Kettering

Rushing towards Kettering
Jamie Mckerral, Kettering

A field near Little Harrowden, November 2007
Derek Chamberlain, Kettering

The River Ise, Isham, February 2007
David Brant, Isham

Trees outside my house on a
foggy afternoon
Elaine Medcalf, Barton Seagrave

East Carlton Countryside
Park, Autumn 2007
Lisa Joy Oliver, Corby

Harringworth Viaduct, New Year's Day 2007
Toby Jewell, Corby

Kelmarsh Hall, February 2008
Mike Camp, Thrapston

A beautiful scene across open
fields in Raunds, November 2007
Garry Chambers, Raunds

Mill Lane, Earls Barton
Robert Ambidge, Earls Barton

Icy, foggy sunset over
Cranford St Andrew
Jane Stonebridge, Cranford

River Nene at Earls Barton
James Spencer, Bozeat

Lyveden New Bield
Steve Bryan, Kettering

View of Loddington
Danielle Kisby, Loddington

At the two bridges near Earls Barton that cross the A45
Robert Ambidge, Earls Barton

74

A pleasant view
Jade Hurst, Wellingborough

A January sunset in Great Doddington
Sam Wood, Great Doddington

Mill Lane, Earls Barton
Robert Ambidge, Earls Barton

The A45 near Earls Barton
Robert Ambidge, Earls Barton

My son and granddaughter at Salcey Forest
Yvonne Kinton, Stanwick

77

Green Lane, Wymington, after the frost
Sarah Woods, Wymington

View from the A14
Ryan Kyle, Kettering

A rainbow over Kettering
Carlene Byland, Kettering

Grafton Underwood
Carlene Byland, Kettering

Wicksteed Park
Carlene Byland, Kettering

Oakley Vale
Bartlomiej Krogulec, Corby

A darkened Corby
Bartlomiej Krogulec, Corby

Stanwick Lakes
Alwyn York, Raunds

Boughton Park, Weekley
Alan Abbott

Near Aldwincle, February 2008
George Reilly, Kettering

Hedgerow on the Benefield/
Weldon Road in January 2008
Peter Lummis, Stanion

84

Kettering Parish Church taken from
the Manor House gardens
Margaret Green, Corby

A view of Warkton
Deb Thurland, Kettering

St Leonard's Church, Rockingham
Neil Jarman, Cottingham

Abington Park, Northampton
Judith Soden, Northampton

Stanwick Lakes
Diana Railton, Woodford

Late summer 2007 at Rothwell North Development Area
David Jones, Rothwell

A bridge near Stanwick Lakes
Diana Railton, Woodford

Fineshade Woods
Shaun Sowell, Kettering

Backwater Fields at Wicksteed Park
J.D. Ashby, Kettering

Campbell Road, Corby, on a summer's day, 2000
Richard Shearer, Corby

Where the rainbow
ends, Hilltop Road,
Little Harrowden
Robert Coles, Little
Harrowden

Willow Place, Corby
T.J. Mears, Corby

Cottingham, overlooking the
Welland Valley, Summer 2007
Chris Brown, Cottingham

Autumn 2007, Cottingham Road,
just before Corby Old Village
T.J. Mears, Corby

Corby Boating Lake, December 2006
Marina Kraan, Corby

Hardwick Church, after a
snowy New Year's Eve
Robert Coles, Little
Harrowden

Ringstead Lake
Elaine Major, Raunds

East Carlton Country Park in Autumn
Tom Redmond, Corby

Snowdrops at Church Lane, Great Cransley
J. Budworth, Kettering

From a lay-by on the A6 near Rushden
Celia Franks, Kettering

Winter's day at the River Nene
Pat Weedy, Higham Ferrers

Fishing at Pitsford
Andrea Flude, Desborough

Wicksteed Park Fishing Lake
Marion Rasheeda Buksh, Kettering

Oakley Hounds at Castle Ashby
Jennifer Spencer, Bozeat

Woodland, near Denford
Peter W. Keep, Stanwick

Sunrise over Braybrooke Road, Desborough
Dot Panter, Melton Mowbray

An old Oak Tree in Lake Avenue, Kettering
Julie Wilson, Kettering

Bridle path to Mawsley
Heather Jackson, Walgrave

From the fields behind St Peter's Church, Irthlingborough
Karl Lamford, Irtlingborough

Sunrise over Kettering
S. Tomlinson, Kettering

Corby Boating Lake,
Winter 2006
Anna Clarke, Corby

Denford, December 2007
Ry Brice, Kettering

100

Hardwater Mill, near Doddington
M.D.B. Dent

Corby Boating Lake
Anna Clarke, Corby

The Green, Orlingbury, Autumn 2007
P.J. White, Orlingbury

Gardens at St Mary's Hospital, Kettering
J.D. Ashby, Kettering

Our little grandson, Archie, at
Wakerley Woods, near Corby
J. Goode, Rothwell

Jack and Gnasher during haytime in the meadow
with Harringworth Viaduct in the background
Sam Boon, Harringworth

My grandson, Ben Clarke, seven, on the zip wire at Barnwell Country Park
Judith Clarke, Barton Seagrave

Chapel Lane, Geddington
E. Drage, Geddington

Sunrise in Corby
Krzysztof Dreczkowski, Corby

Snow scene in Orlingbury
P.J. White, Orlingbury

105

St Botolph's Church, Barton Seagrave
J.D. Ashby, Kettering

Wicksteed Park backwater
J.D. Ashby, Kettering

Sunrise over Finedon Road, Irthlingborough
Ian Kirton, Irthlingborough

Snowdrops at East Carlton
Country Park
Anna Clarke, Corby

Sunset at Rockingham
Krzysztof Dreczkowski, Corby

107

Harringworth Church
Maggie Boon, Harringworth

Looking over Rockingham
Krzysztof Dreczkowski, Corby

108

Orangery at Barton Hall
John Ashby, Kettering

Imaginative
sunset, taken
near West
Haddon
Judith Soden,
Northampton

109

Near Harringworth early one cold and frosty morning in December 2007
Derek Chamberlain, Kettering

110

View from Geddington Bridge, February 2007
Hayley Brown, Geddington

Barton Seagrave sunrise, 2000
John Ashby, Kettering

A Warwickshire & Northamptonshire Air Ambulance
landing in Elizabeth Street, Corby

Lisa Joy Oliver, Corby, with her winning picture

Floods at Harringworth in January
Pauline Boone, Corby

A ghostly figure in the tree,
Great Oakley Church
Robert Scott, Danesholme, Corby

A hunt advances
Steve Bryan, Kettering

Elliott and Oliver Sanders, Ise
Valley in Kettering, following
the flooding of the river
Julian Sanders, Kettering

Floods on the causeway
path across the Nene
Valley, from Higham
Ferrers to Irthlingborough
Will Lovell, Rushden

Express Factory fire, Irthlingborough
Karl Lamford, Irthlingborough

Roofers at Highfield Road,
Wellingborough
A.E. Presland, Wellingborough

Flooding at Geddington, January 2008
Derek Chamberlain, Kettering

Royal British Legion Club fire
Bernie Mills, Corby

The Ise Valley, after the flooding of the river
Julian Sanders, Kettering

My granddaughter, competing at a
meeting at Chelmsford

W.F. Arthur, Broughton, with his winning picture

Grantown Close Sk8
Park, Kettering
Reg Lewin, Kettering

Wellingborough Rugby Club
Alyson Brown, Wellingborough

Miles, in black for S&L under-10s,
is about to score a try
Loraine Mulligan, Corby

Players' eye view: S&L under-10s first match of the season against Oadby.
Loraine Mulligan, Corby

The Parade of Power in Wellingborough, Autumn 2006
Peter Horvath, Wellingborough

Cransley Sailing Club
K.M. Briggs, Rothwell

Junior sailors in a mirror,
Thrapston Sailing Club
Diana Railton, Woodford

Emma, at Thrapston Sailing Club
Diana Railton, Woodford

Sunday fishing on the River Nene
Anna Clarke, Corby

Corby Swimming Baths,
September 2007
Lorraine Dziarkowska, Corby

Taken at the White Water Rafting Centre in Northampton in November 2007
John Woods, Burton Latimer

A Pro40 victory for Northamptonshire
over Hampshire, August 2007
Derek Chamberlain, Kettering

Woodsend Bowling Club, Gainsborough
Road, Corby, Summer 2007
Lisa Joy Oliver, Corby

A tree at Grafton Woods

Jack Fitzhugh, nine, Kettering, with his winning picture

My dog, at home
Andrew Mullin, 15, Corby

Barnwell Country Park, near Oundle
Charles Angus, 11, Kettering

A lovely sunset
Jasmine Wallace, 15, Rothwell

My cat
Jasmine Wallace, 15, Rothwell

Ron the guinea pig
Zach Plumley, 12, Burton Latimer

My cat, Poppy
Kerry White, 17, Catworth

Trees in East Carlton Country Park
Georgiana Angus, nine, Kettering

133

The undergrowth
James Michael Tobin, 15, Rushden

Our dog
Charlotte Lipscombe, 15,
Wellingborough

Sywell Country Park
Brian Forbes, nine, Corby

135

Out at play
James Michael Tobin, 15, Rushden

Setting sun at Earls Barton
Rhia Williams, 16, Earls Barton

A brilliant sunset
James Michael Tobin, 15, Rushden

Scrumpy
Harriet Partridge, 14,
Wellingborough

Mist on the water at Earls Barton Lakes
Rhia Williams, 16, Earls Barton

Walgrave at 5pm in January
Roni Clifford, five, Wellingborough

Sywell Country Park
Brian Forbes, nine, Corby

140

My brother, Jake, playing cricket for Wellingborough
Zoe Westley, nine, Wellingborough

Water at Kelmarsh Hall
Matthew Sharman, 11, Seagrave

A rainbow over Clipstone Court, Rothwell
Amie Jayne Wooton, eight, Rothwell

Boxing Day, Brigstock.
Chelsea Graham, 16, Wellingborough

142

A sunset in Little Cransley
James Watson, nine

at heart 💛 publications

For details of other At Heart books, visit www.atheart.co.uk